is wet boy went dripping home.

This bad boy — this is true.—
Put trick teeth in father's stew!

Gnick-gnack, Paddy wack
Gnasher wants a bone.

Lots of cake and stuff got thrown!

This bad boy cursed and swore,
Asked to push Dad's garden mower.

This bad boy out did drive,
All the bees from father's hive.

Gnick-gnack, Paddy wack
Gnasher wants a bone.

Funny buzzing on the phone?

Turn to inside back
page for more gnick-gnacks—

£3.85

AW! LOOK AT THE QUEUE!

TEN-PIN BOWLING

Q HERE

SPIN
GASP! WHERE DID THAT BOWLING BALL COME FROM?

CLICK! CLICK! CLICK! CLICK! CLICK!
PHEW! THAT BALL'S CERTAINLY KNOCKING THEM DOWN, OK!

HAW-HAW! IT'S GNASHER!

KNOCKING THINGS DOWN IS GREAT FUN!
GRR!

Soon—
NOW FOR ANOTHER KNOCK-DOWN!

IT DOESN'T TAKE MUCH TO KNOCK DOWN THE SOFTIES!
CLAP!
OUCH! WHAT HARD BUBBLES!

At a fun-fair—

HERE'S SOMETHING ELSE TO KNOCK DOWN!

So—

WHIRR!

CRACK!

KNOCK THE CANS DOWN!

OOPS! MISSED!

TOPPLE

HOI!

LOOK, I'VE KNOCKED DOWN THE CANS! DO I GET A PRIZE?

SNARL! YOU PRIZE PEST!

Soon—

£10 TO ANYONE WHO CAN KNOCK DOWN BASHER McTURK!

CAN I HAVE A GO?

THIS ISN'T FOR LITTLE BOYS!

Inside—

TEE-HEE! STOP IT!

TICKLE

SEE! I'VE KNOCKED HIM DOWN WITH A FEATHER! HE'S NOT SO TOUGH!

OO-HOO-HOO-HOO!

Later—

WAIT TILL I CATCH THAT CHEEKY CAT!

RASP!

BIRD BATH

I'LL BE SAFER UP THIS TREE!

GNASH! GNASH!

BET YOU WISH YOU COULD KNOCK DOWN THAT OLD TREE, GNASHER!

HAW-HAW! MAYBE YOU CAN!

CHOMP!

MY FENCE!

CRASH!

BONK!

ERK! DAD!

SO YOU TWO LIKE KNOCKING THINGS DOWN, DO YOU?...

... WELL YOU CAN KNOCK DOWN THESE FENCE POSTS INTO THE GROUND!

PHEW! GASP!

CASTLE HASSLE

THE SOFTY SAVER

IT'S ALL RIGHT! YOU CAN COME OUT — DENNIS HAS GONE SWIMMING!

EH?

SOFTY SAVER SERVICE

PULL

THE POSTIE'S TROUSER REPAIR SHOP

PESKY GNASHER! HE BIT MY TROUSERS AGAIN!

ME TOO!

AND ME!

REPAIRS WHILE U WAIT

THE FAKE DAD MAKER

YOUR DENNIS IS A PEST!

SEND HIM AWAY!

PUNISH HIM!

WHAP

SOLD

SAVES ME A LOT OF TROUBLE!

GET YOUR FAKE DAD HERE

KICK

STOMP

Business

A LOT OF PEOPLE IN BEANOTOWN ARE KEPT IN WORK BECAUSE OF GNASHER AND ME . . .

THE EMERGENCY MOBILE PSYCHIATRIST

CALM DOWN! MAYBE DENNIS WILL BE OFF SCHOOL TODAY!

TREMBLE

SHAKE

SCH

THE CATAPULT AND PEASHOOTER SHOP

WHAT A CUSTOMER!

TUM-TE-TUM!

PEAS

AS

PEAS

PEAS

THE VERY STRONG DOG CLIPPER

NNG! HARD WORK, THIS!

OO—HA-HA-HA! WHAT A GAME! HO-HO-HO!

"IT'S A KNOCKABOUT" IS GREAT FUN! LET'S CHALLENGE THE SOFTIES TO A COMPETITION!

So—

YOU SOFTIES HAVE TO WALK ALONG THE PLANK WITH A BUCKET OF WATER BALANCED ON YOUR HEADS, WHILE WE TRY TO MAKE YOU SPILL IT!

SOUNDS JOLLY FUN!

So—

OUR BALLET TRAINING GIVES US PERFECT BALANCE!

PRANCE

BIG HAIRY SPIDERS!

FIERCE MICE!

CREEPIE CRAWLIES!

SPILL

SPILL

SHAKE

TREMBLE

SHUDDER

SHRIEK! DON'T SAY THOSE WORDS!

And—

PATHETIC! WE'LL BEAT THAT EASILY!

But—

ROGER THE DODGER!

THE BASH STREET KIDS!

BILLY WHIZZ!

HAW-HAW!

HO-HO!

TEE-HEE! THEY ALWAYS LAUGH LIKE THAT AT THE "BEANO" CHARACTERS! WE WIN!

HA! HA!

IF YOU ARE SOMEWHERE YOU DON WANT TO BE, HERE'S MY GUIDE TO GETTIN
THROWN OUT!

1. AT A BORING FILM . . .

. . . GET WALTER TO DO HIS FAMOUS VIKING SHADOW SHOW.

4. AT A CRICKET MATCH . . .

. . . SHOW YOUR HOLIDAY SLIDES ON THE SIGHT SCREENS.

SLIDES

5. IN THE MUSEUM . . .

. . . TRY SOME JOUSTING.

2. AT WIMBLEDON . . .

. . . FEED THE BABY IN THE HIGH CHAIR.

3. AT THE OPERA . . .

BUY SKINNIO SLIMMING FOOD!

. . . SPONSOR A SINGER.

6. IN A CAFE . . .

. . . FIND OUT IF CROISSANTS FLY LIKE BOOMERANGS.

COSY CAFE

KNOCK!

SPLOSH!

BEDTIME STORY

"TIME TO TIDY UP THESE OLD ROSE-PETALS!"

And—

"THERE! THAT'S BETTER!"

COMPOST HEAP →

"ERK! IT'S RASHER!"

"POO! WHAT'S THAT HORRID SWEET SMELL?"

DENNIS'S PET PIG →

"YOU CAN'T "STY" THERE— I'LL FIND YOU A NEW BED!"

"THERE'S A BED FOR YOU—A RIVER BED!"

"GREAT!"

SPLUTCH!

"RASHER LOVES SMELLY MUD!"

But, upstream—

"RIGHT, FRED, OPEN THE SLUICE-GATES!"

SWOOSH!

"OINK!"

SWOOSH!

Little known facts about... SCHOOL

THE WHOLE SCHOOL STAFF WILL FIT INTO THE CUPBOARD IN DENNIS'S CLASSROOM!

PUSH!

THERE ARE 87 DIFFERENT COLOURS OF PAINT IN THE SCHOOL!

SPLAT!

SQUIRT!

ONLY 52 WILL WASH OUT!

SCRUB!

Later—

WOW! I DON'T BELIEVE IT!

OK, WALTER—IF IT'S A FIGHT YOU'RE AFTER...

FIGHTING?.. DON'T BE RIDICULOUS!

I'M HAVING A TEDDY TEA PARTY! THESE GLOVES ARE FOR SAFETY IN CASE I SPILL SOME LUKEWARM TEA ON MY DELICATE HANDIES!

Soon—

EXCELLENT—I SEE YOU'RE BEING SAFETY CONSCIOUS!

THIS RUBBER SUCKER'S NOT FOR SAFETY!

GOT IT!

I'LL HAVE A STROLL ROUND THE GARDEN BEFORE TEA.

ALRIGHT, DEAR.

NOW TO GET THAT APPLE—ERK! DAD! WHERE DID YOU COME FROM?

YOW! MY NOSE!

P-Y-O-N-N-N-G!

SURELY YOU WOULDN'T FIRE AN ARROW WITHOUT SOMETHING ON THE TIP!

THROB THROB

OF COURSE NOT!

HAR-HAR! THAT TIP WASN'T VERY SAFE FOR DENNIS!

TWANG!

WHAP!

HAVING A BALL

SAVE THIS ONE, GNASHER!

KICK

GNASH!

BEAT YOU! I'VE SCORED!

OH, GOSH! IT'S GONE INTO THE SOFTIES' HUT!

SOFTIES' HUT

BONK!

THUMP!

THWACK!

IS THIS YOUR BALL?

YES, WHY?

BECAUSE IT GIVES ME GREATER PLEASURE TO BURST IT IF IT IS!

NO!

BANG!

BANG!

QUICK, CHUMMIES — BOLT THE DOOR!

YOU'VE RUINED IT — POOR BALL! SERVE YOU RIGHT IF IT CAME BACK TO HAUNT YOU!

HEY! THAT'S AN IDEA!

OOH! WE DO ENJOY HARD SUMS.

VERY HARD SUM BOOK

IT'S A PINK ALERT! THAT MEANS A JOB FOR . . .

TINKLE! TINKLE! TINKLE!

FLASH!

VERY HARD SUM BOOK

SOFTY ACTION SQUAD!

S.A.S.

S.A.S.

S.A.S.

S.A.S.

WHAT'S THAT, REXYKINS? OH! HOW AWFUL!

FRIGHTFUL NEWS, CHAPPIES! NERVOUS REX HAS HAD A HAIR BLOWN OUT OF PLACE ON HIS WAY TO EXTRA TUITION!

GASP!

HOW HORRID!

INTO ACTION, MEN! READY, STEADY . . .

But—

PRESENTATION SENSATION

ABOUT THIS TIME OF YEAR WE PRESENT OUR "MENACE OF THE YEAR" AWARD!

ABOUT THIS TIME OF YEAR WE PRESENT OUR "SOFTY OF THE YEAR" AWARD!

SOFTY OF THE YEAR

GNASHER DID SOME MENACING IN THE SUMMER...

CUT THE HEDGE FOR ME, GNASHER.

CHOMP! GNASH!

DAD WON'T TRY THAT AGAIN TEE-HEE!

DAD IS A LAZY BLOB

SHRIEK!

GOING INTO BAT, SPOTTY?

OH, NO...

SPOTTY WAS VERY SOFT AT ONE CRICKET MATCH!

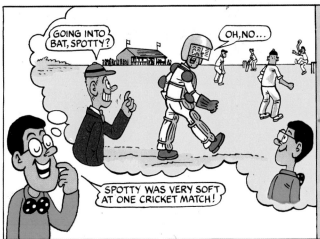

...I'M SCORER! DANGEROUS JOB— YOU NEVER KNOW WHEN A PENCIL POINT MIGHT BREAK AND HIT YOU!

THAT'S TRUE! HOW BRAVE YOU ARE!

REMEMBER WHEN DENNIS CHANGED ROUND A DIRECTION POST?...

DOG POUND CAT SHOW

And—

GREAT PIECE OF MENACING, THAT!

GROWL! SNARL!

SQUEAL!

I RECALL WHEN WALTER HAD TO SLEEP ON THE FLOOR...

...BECAUSE HIS BED WAS SO FULL OF TEDDIES AND CUDDLY TOYS!

PIE-FACE DID SOME BRILLIANT MENACING TO THE BRASS BAND!

HEH-HEH!

PIES

PIE

SILENCE

WHAT ABOUT WHEN BERTIE SPENT ALL HIS MONEY ON A CRASH-HELMET TO PROTECT HIM FROM NASTY, HEAVY SNOWFLAKES?

EEK!

WAH!

ERK!

DO YOU REMEMBER WHEN CURLY PUT ITCHING POWDER IN THE SOFTIES' DANCING PUMPS?

I'M THE MOST MENACING!

AND I'M THE SOFTEST!

I'LL WIN!

SO WILL I!

DENNIS! WHAT'S ALL THE NOISE ABOUT?

DAD'S VOICE
OO-ER! TIME WE WERE OFF!

IT'S BAD ENOUGH HAVING TO MODEL FOR MUM'S NEW DRESS WITHOUT ALL THIS NOISE!

HE FRIGHTENED DENNIS AWAY!

ER-FOR ME?

SOFTEST OUTFIT I'VE EVER SEEN!

TIME

For this, menacing game you'll need tiddlywinks or buttons. Put your Dennis Book on the floor open at this page and try to feed Gnasher and Gnipper by landing counters in their mouths. Each player's turn consists of three shots with the first to score 50 points the winner. Score the highest number that the counter touches. Fire from one Softy Width away (about 1.5 very soft metres). Happy tiddling!

LOSE 5pts IF YOU LAND IN WALTER'S PRETTY BUTTON BOX.

10 pts

2 pts FOR A NEAR MISS

Soon—

LET ME AT THEM!

BETTER TAKE ANOTHER DETOUR!

SUPERB PIE COMPANY

Later—

PHEW! WE MUST HAVE BEEN WALKING FOR MILES. LET'S FIND A SEAT SOMEWHERE.

AT LEAST WE'VE KEPT PIE-FACE AWAY FROM ANY PIES!

WHAT'S THAT PLEASANT SOUND I HEAR?

DING-DONG!

OH, NO! IT CAN'T BE!

AFTER ALL WE'VE DONE TO KEEP PIE-FACE AWAY FROM PIES...

BILL'S GIANT PIES

... THE PIES COME TO PIE-FACE!

Just in time—

CLANG!

WELL DONE, GNASHER!

← READER'S VOICE

At the fair—

"NAME THAT PIE" COMPETITION PRIZES GALORE

I DON'T SUPPOSE PICTURES OF PIES CAN DO MUCH HARM!

I MUST TRY THIS!

PORK – APPLE – CHICKEN – SHEPHERD'S – BILBERRY – MUD – MINCE – STEAK AND KIDNEY – HAM AND SEMOLINA – BLACKBIRD!

HERE'S YOUR PRIZE! WELL DONE, SON!

ASSORTED PIES

HE'S DONE IT AGAIN!

HEY! THOSE PIES ARE MINE!

CHOMP! GUZZLE! WE MUST FINISH THESE BEFORE PIE-FACE GETS FREE! CHEW! CHOMP!

CHOMP! SLURP!

Next day—

HEY! WHY SO SAD, PIE-FACE?

← READER'S VOICE

BECAUSE I'M ALL ALONE TODAY!

TUT-TUT! VERY BAD CASES ALL OF YOU!

YOU CAN GUESS WHAT THEY'VE GOT, CAN'T YOU, READERS?

THE BOY'S GOT BOTTLE

STONE CROWS

DID I EVER TELL YOU ABOUT THE TIME A SHORT-SIGHTED MOTHER CROW THOUGHT I WAS ONE OF HER BROOD..?

POOR CHILD! FELL OUT OF OUR NEST, DID YOU?

GNEEK!

HUH! NO CHANCE OF GETTING ANY BONES UP HERE!

Soon—

YEUCH! I'M GOING TO SNEAK AWAY AND CALL FOR HELP!

GASP! THIS IS TRICKY! FAIRLY TAKES YOUR BREATH AWAY!

But then—

PANT! I'LL HIDE IN HERE—GASP!—TILL I RECOVER—THEN I'LL GIVE DENNIS'S DAD A YELL!

And—

LET'S INSULT GNASHER! HE'LL BE IN HIS KENNEL—AND WE'RE SAFE UP HERE!

GNASHER'S A SOFTY DOG!

BOO TO YOU, SOFTY GNASHER!

TEE-HEE! I'M ENJOYING THIS!

YES—GOOD JOB GNASHER CAN'T CLIMB TREES!

GNASH!

YIKES!

BUT...EEK!

GNASH! GNASH!

EH?

WHAT?

HOW'D HE GET UP HERE?

HOW'D HE GET UP HERE?

MAYBE A LITTLE BIRD WILL TELL THEM! GNEE! GNEE!

Dennsil and Gnashtel

(A MENACING FAIRY STORY)

Once upon a time there were two children, Dennsil and Gnashtel. Their mother didn't like them very much. Dennsil she didn't like because he was always in trouble. Gnashtel she didn't like because he was covered in black hair and always bit the postman. This was quite natural as he was a dog but she was pretty dense and hadn't realised this.

Anyway, she didn't like them, so she sent them out to walk in the woods hoping they would get lost or perhaps eaten by a very large hamster (see — told you she was thick).

FOOD SHOP

The woods were pretty thick too and soon Dennsil and Gnasthel WERE lost. They wandered about for hours getting more and more hungry. There were plenty of fruit trees and even some food shops in the woods but since Dennsil only ever ate sweets and Gnashtel preferred posties' trousers, this was not a lot of help to them.

The wood they were in was a strange place with some very odd buildings in it. King Tredbert the Trampolinist had his bouncy castle there. This was far bigger than those things you see at fairgrounds these days. This one was big enough to hold seven Queens, 52 Princes and Princesses, 104 Dukes, 207 Lords and two overworked servants, every one of them sea sick from Tredbert's non stop trampolining. There was also a library made entirely of books, from which you could borrow real bricks. The sauna bath made from butter had unfortunately melted by the time Dennsil and Gnashtel arrived.

BOUNCE!

SAUNA

Dennsil and Gnashtel wer delighted. They tried the knocker to se if anyone was at home. The knocker wa made of marshmallow and made no sound at all as it knocked against th peanut brittle door. No one answere (you will be surprised to hear) so the did what people always do when no on answers a door — they began to eat th house.

FLUMP! FLUMP!

GNASH! RIP!

GNOW!

OW! OW! OW!

Soon, though, they came to one of the oddest buildings in the wood. It was a house made out of sweets and posties' trousers. The walls were chocolate pebble dashed with mint humbugs, the slates on the roof were crisps, the liquorice chimney puffed out candyfloss smoke and round the doors were pillars of posties' trousers.

They chomped away merrily until they could eat no more. The house was hardly touched. A house will feed two boys (even if one is a dog) for a long long time. Eating too much of it at once will only give you a sore stomach. Dennsil and Gnashtel had found this out and lay groaning on the ground. "Ow! Ow! Ow!" said Dennsil. "Gnow! Gnow! Gnow!" said Gnashtel who spoke in a very odd way.

This groaning was far louder than the sound of the marshmallow door knocker. So loud that it woke up the owner of the house who had been fast asleep inside all along. He came outside to see what was going on. He was not at all pleased when he found out. He jumped up and down shouting at Dennsil and Gnashtel — just like you would do if you found someone eating your house. The next thing you would do is call the police but in fairy tales things are done differently. The man in the house decided the best way to punish them was to put them in the oven and bake them into a pie. Very odd!

He didn't think so, though, and in no time Dennsil and Gnashtel were inside his oven.

MELT

NOOM!

The man turned the fruit drop knob to turn the chocolate oven on and sat back to wait for his pie to cook.

It is one thing to build a house of sweets and posties' trousers, but making an oven out of chocolate is just silly. Almost as soon as it was switched on it melted. Dennsil and Gnashtel were covered in soft chocolate and emerged from the wreck of the oven looking like a pair of very nasty space aliens from the planet Chocco. The owner of the house took one look at them and ran screaming into the woods roaring "Help! I'm being pursued by two space aliens from the planet Chocco!"

Many weird things went on in this wood but no one was going to believe that kind of rubbish, so the man was soon locked up in a home for liars who told particularly large whoppers, where he stayed for the rest of his life.

But what of Dennsil and Gnashtel?

Once they had licked the chocolate off, Dennsil and Gnashtel lived happily ever after in the house made of sweets until one day they ate through the foundations and the whole lot collapsed on them.

HOME for LIARS

CRUMP!

WHAT A LOAD OF RUBBISH

IT'S AMAZING THE THINGS YOU FIND AT THE DUMP!

DUMP

I'LL USE THESE FOR MENACING WITH!

Later—

JUST THROW OUT THESE LEFT-OVERS.

EEK!

-KICK

PYONNG!

TEE-HEE!

GNASHEE!

RASHER— PET PIG

GUZZLE! CHOMP!

Little known facts about... SOFTY WALTER

DENNIS CAN KNOCK OVER WALTER FROM 20 PACES BY PULLING A FACE!

BOOO!

FAINT!

THE LESSER SOFTYPLANT CAN WATER ITSELF!

SOB!

WALTER IS VERY FOND OF THE COLOUR PINK

WALTYPOOHS! WHERE ARE YOU?

GNASHER SHOULD LIKE THIS, TOO!

POWDERED BONES

I'LL MIX IT IN WITH THE REST OF THE STUFF!

POWDERED BONES

GNASHER

GNARGH!

GNASHER

ERK!

GNASTY!

NOW I SEE! YOU'VE BEEN FEEDING GNASHER CAT FOOD!

GULP!

POWDERED FISH BONES

JUST A MINUTE! I'LL BE ABLE TO MAKE AN ADVERT AFTER ALL!

Soon—

WHIRR!

RESEARCH

THAT DOG FOOD'S DONE WONDERS FOR THE DAFFODILS!

"GNASHO-GNOSH" PLANT FOOD WILL MAKE YOUR GARDEN GROW!

GNASHO GNOSH

GNESH!

OH FOR THE WINGS OF A DOG!

SUPER! AREN'T BUTTERFLIES AMAZING? SUCH GRACE! SUCH BEAUTY!

FLUTTER

DENNIS'S DAD

SUCH SOPPINESS!

WALTER, PRINCE OF SOFTIES

GNESH!

DID YOU KNOW THAT IN SOUTH AMERICA THEY HAVE GIANT BUTTERFLIES?...

WISH HE'D SHUT UP ABOUT BUTTERFLIES— SOFT THINGS!

A-Z OF BUTTER FLIES

I KNOW HOW TO PUT WALTER OFF BUTTERFLIES!

LINEN CUPBOARD

THAT'S THE WAY, GNASHER!

SQUEEZE

Later, at Walter's house—

HEY, WALTER— ONE OF THOSE GIANT BUTTERFLIES MUST HAVE COME OVER TO BRITAIN AND LAID ITS EGGS!

WHAT MAKES YOU SAY THAT?

THAT MUST BE ONE OF ITS CATERPILLARS!

SQUEAL! A HORRID CREEPIE-CRAWLIE!

SLITHER

CLEVER PICTURE QUIZ

THESE DRAWINGS REPRESENT? (ANSWERS AT FOOT OF PAGE)

IN THE PARK—

LOVELY MUD!

OOPS! CAN'T STOP!

MY BACK'S KILLING ME, PICKING UP THIS LITTER!

YOUR PROBLEM'S SOLVED!

A HAM ROLL!

LITTER

THIS IS FOR YOUR PIG'S HELP!

COO! THANKS!

LITTER

PICK

WONDER IF THERE'S ANY MOULDY COMPOST IN WALTER'S GARDEN?

THUNDER!

LITTLE SOFT BOY

SQUIRT!

ERK!

OIL

BUMP!

OUT OF MY WAY!

SPLUDGE!

I'M FROM THE FAIRGROUND. CAN I HIRE YOUR PIG?

WHINE!

EH? SURE!

AND—

GREASY PIG

10p A RIDE

CASH

NOW I'VE GOT MONEY FOR MYSELF AND ENOUGH TO BUY YOU A SLAP-UP FEED!

OINK!

GNASH!

IN A POSH RESTAURANT—

I'LL READ OUT THE MENU—YOU GRUNT TO TELL ME WHAT YOU WANT!

LOVELY FLOWERS!

HOTEL POSH MENU

SCOTCH BROTH, MELON, STEAK PIE, SPAGHETTI, FISH AND CHIPS, CUSTARD, PRUNES RHUBARB TART

HOTEL POSH MENU

GRUNT! GRUNT! GRUNT! GRUNT! GRUNT! GRUNT! GRUNT! GRUNT!

THAT GREEDY PIG'S EATING ALL THE FOOD TOGETHER! HOW DISGUSTING!

CHOMP!

GORGE!

BONES AND CHIPS

CRUNCH! GNASH!

LITTLE SOFT CHAPPIE

CHESS SET

LOOK AT ALL THE TOYS WALTER GOT FOR PASSING HIS EXAMS.

ALL I GOT FOR *NOT* PASSING WAS A WHACKING FROM DAD!

HEAT FROM WHACKING

I KNOW—I'LL MAKE MY OWN TOYS!

HOW DO YOU LIKE MY PORTRAIT OF DEAR FLUFFY?

PURR-FECT!

I'D LIKE TO SHOW IT TO SOMEONE!

LOOK, GNASHER!

SNARL!

GNASH!

GNASH!

GNASH!

GNASH!

GREAT JIGSAW PUZZLE, THIS!

Little known facts about...

GNASHER and GNIPPER

THE POSTIE WHO DELIVERS TO THEIR HOUSE HAS 102 UNIFORMS — ALL WITH THE LEGS GNASHED!

...OAD'S GARDEN NOW CONTAINS MORE BONES THAN SOIL!

THE RECORD NUMBER OF CATS UP A TREE IS 243!

Later... Walter's turn to bat—

WHIMPER! DON'T BOWL TOO HARD NOW!

TAP!

OOOH!

TOPPLE

OUT! HOW PATHETIC!

YOU BOWL!

HORRORS! NO! NO! I CAN'T DO THAT!

WHY NOT, FOR GOODNESS SAKE?

I COULDN'T FORGIVE MYSELF IF I CRUSHED ONE OF THOSE LOVELY DAISIES!

WHY NOT WORK THE SCOREBOARD?

SCOREBOARD

VERY WELL.

SCOREBOARD

IDIOT! YOU'RE MEANT TO KEEP THE SCORE—NOT DO SUMS!

YOU BE UMPIRE—HERE—KEEP MY JERSEY!

AND MINE!

HOWZAT?

ZZZ!

WAKEN UP!

HELP! WHAT? I WAS SO LOVELY AND COSY I FELL ASLEEP!

HOW DID YOU GET ON PLAYING WITH WALTER?

HIM? HE'S JUST A MENACE!

WALTER—A MENACE? GASP!

THE SHAME!

HEH-HEH!

Little known facts about... RASHER

TAKE THAT ANIMAL TO THE MARKET! YOU'LL HAVE TO SELL HIM TO PAY ALL THE BILLS!

SOB! SOB!

At the market—

HM! I'VE AN IDEA!

ROLL UP! ROLL UP! HOOPLA— 10p A GO!

Later—

HIT THE HEADS! 10p-3 THROWS

SPLAT!

SPLAT!

GROAN! NOW TO CLEAR THIS LOT UP!

RASHER WON'T TAKE LONG TO CLEAN IT UP!

WOW! THANKS! HERE'S A REWARD!

CHOMP!

GUZZLE!

I'M FED UP OF THIS—I'M NOT MOVING!

PORKER DONKEY RIDES 10p

THUD!

ME FIRST!

PORKER DONKEY RIDES 10p

POULTRY CABBAGES

YAHOO! BETTER THAN A DONKEY ANY DAY!

WAHEY!

Back home—

I GOT ENOUGH MONEY TO PAY THE BILLS AND TO BUY SOMETHING AT THE MARKET!

REALLY? WHAT DID YOU GET?

Dad

RIGHT LITTLE MENACES, EH, DAD?

SQUEAL!

CHOMP! GUZZLE!

CHOMP!

CHOMP!

Dad

MUST KEEP TRYING!

HEY! WHAT'S THAT THE SOFTIES ARE SHAKING OVER ONE ANOTHER?

GREAT! MAYBE IT'S PEPPER!

EEK!

HUH! IT'S NOT PEPPER...

SCREECH TO HALT

...IT'S PERFUMED TALCUM POWDER. I MIGHT HAVE KNOWN!

TEE-HEE! SERVES YOU RIGHT!

REEL

OH, BOTHER! MY CONTINENTAL QUILT'S BURST!

OH-OH!

IT—IT'S GOING TO WORK!

ATCHOO!

JUST IN TIME. MY NOSE HAS BEEN BLOCKED ALL MORNING—AND IT'S NOT NEARLY SO MUCH FUN COMING HOME FOR LUNCH IF YOU CAN'T SMELL WHAT MUM'S COOKING FOR YOU!

Later— I'M THE FINEST BATTER AROUND

THWACK!

SHOW-OFF!

YAH! BET I COULD KNOCK YOUR MIDDLE STUMP OUT!

PIFFLE!

YOU WON'T EVEN SEE THE BALL!

SWIPE

ERK!

GREAT BALL, DENNIS!

HE'S RIGHT! I DIDN'T SEE IT!

THAT'S TAKEN THE WIND OUT OF HIS SAILS!

SHAME

HEH! HEH! I DIDN'T NEED TO USE A BALL—JUST A MOLE!

Back home—

A MOLE'S BEEN EATING OUR CARROTS.

I'LL DIG IT OUT.

TIME YOU WERE OFF!

OOER! I'M AWAY!

Next door—

ISN'T MY CLOCKWORK TRAIN SPIFFING?

ABSOLUTELY SUPER!

CHUG! CHUG!

YIKES!

IT'S AFTER ME!

WHERE IS THAT MOLE?

EEK!

MY, MY! DELIVERED BY UNDERGROUND RAILWAY!

This bad boy, up to tricks,
Blocked up the front door with bricks.

GNASH! GNASH!

WOBBLE

Gnick-gnack, Paddy wack
Gnasher wants a bone.

CHOCS

Mum's quite happy o[n] [her]
own!

CLUNK

KICK

Used a ball he'd carved from stone.

PUMP
PUMP

This bad boy thinks its great,
Spotty Perkins to inflate.

PTCHEEE

PLOP

BOING

Gnick-gnack, Paddy wack
Gnasher wants a bone.

GURGLE   BURBLE

BURBLE

GURGLE

Menace house engulfed by foam!

This bad boy runs off, then,